A
LIFE-ALTERING
JOURNEY

JOYCE M. BEATTY

A LIFE-ALTERING JOURNEY
By Joyce M. Beatty

Copyright © 2018 by Joyce M. Beatty

ISBN: 978-1-949297-05-8
LCCN: 2018948967

Unless otherwise noted, all scriptures are from the KING JAMES VERSION, public domain.

Scripture quotations marked (NIV) are from the Holy Bible, NEW INTERNA-TIONAL VERSION®. Copyright © 1973, 1978, 1984, 2011 by Biblica, Inc.™. Used by permission of Zondervan.

Scripture quotations marked (NKJV) are taken from the NEW KING JAMES VERSION®. Copyright © 1982 by Thomas Nelson, Inc. Used by permission. All rights reserved.

Scripture quotations marked (AMP) are taken from the AMPLIFIED® BIBLE. Copyright © 1954, 1958, 1962, 1964, 1965, 1987 by the Lockman Foundation. Used by permission. (www.Lockman.org).

Scripture quotations marked (NLT) are taken from THE HOLY BIBLE, NEW LIVING TRANSLATION. Copyright © 1996, 2004, 2007 by Tyndale House Foundation. Used by permission of Tyndale House Publishers, Inc., Carol Stream, Illinois 60188. All rights reserved. Used by permission.

Address all personal correspondence to:

Joyce M. Beatty
Email: gbeatty@ec.rr.com

Individuals and church groups may order books from Joyce M. Beatty directly, or from the publisher. Retailers and wholesalers should order from our distributors. Refer to the Deeper Revelation Books website for distribution information, as well as an online catalog of all our books.

Published by:

Deeper Revelation Books
Revealing "the deep things of God" (1 Cor. 2:10)
P.O. Box 4260
Cleveland, TN 37320
Phone: (423) 478-2843
Website: www.deeperrevelationbooks.org
Email: info@deeperrevelationbooks.org

Deeper Revelation Books assists Christian authors in publishing and distributing their books. Final responsibility for design, content, permissions, editorial accuracy, and doctrinal views, either expressed or implied, belongs to the author.

Table of Contents

Appreciation

This writing is a labor of love dedicated to the memory of my God-fearing parents Luther and Vina McKoy, my sister and best friend Vee, my husband Gerald, my children Wendy, Michael and Brandon, my grandchildren Calyn, Jasmine and Michaela, my siblings, and to all the others who loved me enough to speak truth in my life.

Prologue

Most of us look forward to the blessings from the Lord. Few rejoice in the labor and perseverance required to make the journey through the highways and hedges to fulfill the great commission of sharing the good news, the gospel of Jesus Christ. I pray that my story will inspire you to take a greater stand for the cause of the Cross.

The following stories are authentic experiences from my life and some lessons learned. My hope is that readers find them informative and thought-provoking, resulting in a deeper interest to explore God's Word.

SECTION I

Stories:
GROWING UP

As a little country girl, it was euphoric to sit in the top of a huge chinaberry tree and look out over my world. Everything seemed a little smaller and less formidable. My seven-year-old eagle eyes were full of awe. I was breathlessly exhilarated by the magical view. I could fantasize to my heart's content until jerked back into reality by the fact that I had to descend that huge tree. It was much easier and far more exciting to climb that old tree but frightening and difficult to get back to the ground, especially since I had been forbidden to climb in the first place.

Had I not been such a tomboy, my cute little homemade dresses would have remained intact. But one torn dress and two scarred knees later, not to mention an encounter with one very upset, stern, tired and over-worked mother, I found myself in a pickle that remains a vivid memory to this day because Mother scolded and punished me. Of course, I promised tearfully not to ever follow those boys in their antics again. However, my promise not to climb trees did not last. The tomboy in me just could not be contained. Little did I know that the persistence of a child to out-maneuver my male playmates in climbing trees, shooting marbles, memorizing car styles, and other tomboyish antics would help to build a foundation of perseverance that would help me to excel later in life, a life that would present tests and trials that would require much stamina and faith.

The drive to be successful in whatever endeavor I faced resulted from the foundation provided by my parents. They were God-fearing, hardworking people. Mom and Dad had two generations of children together, six boys and six girls. I came along toward the end, as the 11th child, born on the 11th day of the 11th month. I was even born with 11 fingers, but my mom wisely had the extra removed. We lived in a poor North Carolina county where most families grew crops and raised livestock. Our family was wealthy in values and love for each other, but not in terms of material possessions. Our old house was not much to look at, but it provided a clean shelter for us and was bursting at the seams with joy and love.

My parents, though limited in resources, were industrious. I grew up with my parents, three brothers, and a younger sister. My seven older siblings were residing on their own in other cities. They became relevant to me as they visited the family during their vacations.

Fantasizing, like I did in the chinaberry tree, made childhood in an impoverished, boring country region seem more interesting. If nothing was going on, I would create excitement through fantasy. My world was full of characters from TV, books, and my own imagination that brought excitement to my day.

Fantasy helped me to dream beyond what I could see in the countryside, and in the country school where I was academically ahead of most of my classmates and genuinely bored. Careers for people in my community were teachers, preachers, morticians, farmers, and factory workers. I wanted to be neither. I had grand ideas of moving out and up to so much bigger and better. Ordinary was not for me, but I could never have imagined the path I would follow.

My first educational opportunity was provided in 1968, when the integration of schools could no longer be denied. Although school integration presented opportunities as well as challenges, I got to compete with the brightest students. I learned that there were always challenges beyond my scope of expertise, yet I could still succeed. I learned that my goals were not challenging enough because the world held far more than my previous window of exposure. I wanted to experience that new world and enjoy some of its advantages.

Along the way I learned that not every face was friendly; some did not see my worth and abilities or perhaps did not want to acknowledge them. That did not deter me. I was on a mission and not to be stopped. My commonplace world of poverty, albeit with much love and spiritual guidance, just did not compare to that of my peers who lived on the best side of the tracks in their huge houses with sparkling chandeliers and foyers the size of my bedroom. I could only imagine what life on the other side was like. If vision boards had been in place back then, mine would have exploded with my dreams.

I was an avid reader from the early grades. I read everything I got my hands on. I wanted and craved knowledge. I wanted to know what the world had to offer. I soon learned that college would be my spring board to the better life I sought. It was miraculous that I made it through four years there, since I was solely responsible for my college tuition and other necessities. While parents were dropping their sons and daughters off on campus, I arrived by Greyhound bus, then took a cab with my suitcases, struggling to get to my dorm. Our family's automobile would not have made it to Durham, North Carolina. Through a series of miracles that I can see now, I excelled through hard work and because God put people in my path to direct and assist in some way. Campus work study jobs, summer jobs, scholarships and grants, and having other family who resided an hour away to assist, helped me to make it through those four years.

Like most new college graduates, especially in the late 70s, my expectation was that there would be better jobs and more variety in the job market. Unfortunately, that was not my fate. The country was in a mild recession, and the job market was nothing like I had imagined. Consequently, I did the unthinkable and returned to my hometown. Returning home was not in my original plan, but since I had eloped and married my boyfriend from back home at the beginning of my senior year, my dreams had to be put on hold for many years. Soon I began to again create a fantasy world in my mind to cope with the detour that I willingly created.

Usually, the new college graduate feels that the world will be at her feet, eager to embrace her knowledge and skills. I certainly thought so until I realized that the economy was in a slump, and jobs were difficult to find. My first four years after college graduation were spent working as an executive secretary, a job located through a temp agency.

It was quite a blow to my enthusiastic view of the world, since those in the same position had business certificates rather than four-year degrees. Having to work in a position that did not require a college degree hit my ego and affected my self-esteem. I knew I needed to work; being a snob and unemployed would not pay our bills. My new boss was a cigar-smoking older man who could not keep a good secretary. He was horrific to work for and seemed to enjoy being ornery. However, the persistent country girl who grew up with strong values and determination had surfaced to put her stake in the ground. I was going to be successful until something better came along, no matter what.

It was not unusual for my boss to call me in his office to prepare correspondence five minutes before the end of the day. I felt it was done maliciously since he was usually sitting staring out the window the last hour of the day. Doing so caused me to miss the bus, which was my transportation home.

In the winter months, I waited at least an hour in the dark until the next bus came along because we only had one automobile.

I was determined that I was not going to quit my job. I persevered and remained in the position, until finally my boss retired and was replaced by a kinder, more reasonable employer. Even then, I knew in my heart that God had better for me. I was willing to wait my turn.

Approximately two years later on a Sunday afternoon, I received a phone call about a middle school teaching position. In college I had majored in business with a minor in education. Having completed my student teaching in a school with high crime and lack of discipline, I was reluctant to work in a school immediately after graduation. Even if I had maintained a strong desire to teach after graduation, it would not have mattered since there were no jobs available. The phone call came at a time when I was ready for a change—I now had a different perspective. As a young parent I desired more, a better life for myself and family. It was unusual because the interview occurred over the phone. The remaining process was just a formality. I knew God had intervened on my behalf, so I thought I could finally feel secure and confident as a respected teacher.

My first year as a teacher was the hardest. The system did not have a curriculum or materials for the new program I was hired to teach. Having to develop every part of the instruction from my background and experience, as well as encourage student interest, was most taxing. I worked every evening, weekend, and during the holidays just to stay abreast of the motivated, high-level students assigned to me, and devoting that much time affected my family life.

Even though the process improved over time, other concerns manifested. It was a time of uncertainty due to budget shortfalls. Although I had considered acquiring a new certification and applying to graduate school to make myself more marketable, I did not have the courage or faith that I could pass the graduate exam to move forward.

Old fears and doubts weighed me down. Having told myself numerous times that I would fail the entrance exam, my insecurities got the best of me, and I just felt stuck. I did not know what to do next; it was a low time in my life. I still presented myself to others as secure and happy. As far as anyone knew, my world was progressive and secure. Inside, though, I was fearful, apprehensive and unsure if I would actually have employment the next year. The only person I could be truthful with was Jesus.

Opportunities were available to me. I knew it and went after them, but for some reason, they kept slipping through my fingers. I made sure my supervisor was aware of my interest in transferring to another position. In fact, I wrote a formal letter requesting a transfer to a sought-after position for which I qualified. Several positions became available, but I received no response to my inquiries.

I did not give up, because I wanted a change. I could visualize myself operating successfully in the new assignment and was almost giddy waiting for my special phone call. It was like knowing my ship was out there in the ocean, and would come ashore at some point, but I was uncertain about when it would dock. I was starting to create a fantasy world to accommodate and suppress the disappointment.

Finally, I dusted off those dreams I had tucked away and began praying for help. I had exhausted my other options. Despite us and our weaknesses, God is faithful and desires to bless us more than we know.

Seven years later, my supervisor walked into my classroom to offer me the very position that I had applied for years before. I still wanted the position just as much, but I had come to a place in my life where I had learned to be content where I found myself until God brought forth my change. During that time, I had developed more faith and a greater relationship with my Lord.

I was ecstatic over my blessing from God, but I was still expecting the new position to fill the voids in my life and catapult me to extreme contentment. I worked hard and was faithful in my assignment, but the more fulfilling my employment, the more unhappy my home life seemed to be. I would find myself wondering and fantasizing about happiness for the next 25 years as I strived to be the best mother, best wife, involved Christian, supportive daughter, and more.

I soon found myself locked in a web of being the person to count on for family, friends, and neighbors. I was the one who agreed to take the neighbors' screaming toddlers to daycare since it was on my way to work. I was the one to help with committees and other functions most folks scurried away from. I did not do these deeds for recognition or because I was such a great person, I did them out of insecurity and low self-esteem—my inability to say no.

A typical day after work for me during that time was picking up my children after school, dropping my daughter off for dance practice, rushing home to feed my son a snack and dropping him off at the ball park for little league, returning home to begin dinner preparation, driving back to the dance studio to pick up my daughter, completing dinner, then picking up my son, feeding the children, doing homework, getting baths, doing my chores, staying up late to grade papers, and more. My spouse worked shifts at the time, and our schedules seldom blended. Oftentimes, I stayed up late after everyone was in bed just to unwind and enjoy a moment of escape.

While I was giving my all to others, I had no idea that I was losing myself and becoming an embittered angry mother and wife. The changes began subtly. I would find myself murmuring under my breath as I did laundry or dinner or ran errands. Issues at home that were usually overlooked became more disconcerting, and I was forced to examine my life more closely. No amount of fantasy could transform my reality. I could easily revamp my extracurricular activities and rearrange the schedules of the kids. I could not, however, remove the unhappiness that emanated from the fact that our two-parent family operated as if it was a one-parent family. It was less about work schedules and more about not understanding the value and significance of family, the emotional and spiritual needs of the children, and the partnership of marriage. Over time, there would be major conflict that impacted the stability of our family.

Dishearteningly, it did not seem as if my spouse and I shared the same revelation. I was preoccupied with my responsibilities that seldom included him, and he was tasked with providing for our family and serving as the crusader for his extended family. It did not help that we saw each other less often due to his working shifts.

As we drifted farther and farther apart, I found solace in attending church and nurturing our children. I wrongfully assumed that we would find our way around the iceberg in our lives eventually and without major incident. Unfortunately, he later began to detest me and my relationship with my church family. It became a throbbing, vibrant wall between us resulting in marital separation. As a result, I became bitter and even more disconnected. I could not understand why God would allow this to happen, especially since I was so involved in serving Him.

My deliverance and change of heart that allowed me to catch a glimpse of God's plan for us began the morning after my spouse was no longer in our home. When I woke up, still in shock that he was no longer with us, and just when I was about to put my feet on the floor, the Holy Spirit spoke vibrantly and authoritatively to me: "I will keep thee in perfect peace, he whose mind is stayed on me" (based on Isaiah 26:3). The Word became my anchor then and still is today.

Those words were so alive that it appeared as if they were standing in front of me. It is difficult to express how the "living Word" could appear. I saw nothing, but the Life Giver was there. He never left my side during those long months. My heart changed. The religious layers that I did not know were there began to fall away, and I was willing to learn how to live and be the wife and mother I was called to be. I could finally be a willing conduit for God to work through to save my family. After all, I had the best teacher, Holy Spirit, who continues to teach, guide and chasten as needed.

Marriage is significant to God, and my marriage is highlighted throughout this book because the revolutionary changes that occurred in our marriage not only affected me and my spouse but also continue to impact my family, friends, and everyone else we encounter.

SECTION I

Lesson:
FORGIVENESS

I am a woman of faith today and have been for some 30-plus years. What exactly does that mean? I am a Christian woman who was raised with strong Christian values. I respect the rights of others to believe whatever they choose. However, I believe solidly in Christianity, that Jesus is the Son of God. He is my Lord and Savior.

I strive to follow Proverbs 3:6 which states, "In all thy ways, acknowledge him, and he shall direct thy paths." Prayer is a lifestyle for me. I pray consistently, seeking the Lord for guidance in my life and the lives of others. My Christian relationship helps me to forgive some of the seemingly unforgivable behaviors I have experienced. I don't always get it right, but I am humble enough to forgive as well as ask for forgiveness.

It is a struggle to let go of the emotion that

comes when someone deliberately wrongs or mistreats you, but true Christians are forgiven souls who are not better than others. We should be willing to let go of the wrongs done to us because of the great mercy and grace we have experienced, so we can continue to receive from God even when our lives are in error.

Honestly, I have had no problem in the past harboring dislike and oftentimes pure hatred and bitterness in my heart for those who wronged me. Nevertheless, once I gained an understanding of the power of forgiveness, the liberty it gave me was beyond words.

It became personal and life-changing when in prayer many years ago, Holy Spirit said to me, "You always seek me for forgiveness, yet you are not willing to forgive." At that moment I had a revelation of the power of forgiveness and a deeper understanding of the power of the Cross.

God is faithful. I experience His faithfulness daily. I have come to understand that nothing I could ever do would stop Him from loving me. He just loves His creation. Since He loves us so much, and because we are imperfect humans with a sin nature, God provided a provision for humanity to rectify wrongs. It is called repentance. If I am truly sorry for my wrong deed, I can go to God and ask for forgiveness. If I wronged someone, and it is possible to correct it, I also go to the person and ask their forgiveness. Whether my apology is accepted or not does not change my responsibility to make every attempt to correct my error.

I have been disappointed by people and learned to eventually let it go, but the most difficult times in my life with forgiveness were with my spouse. I made a promise to myself that I would never forgive my spouse for leaving our home. I felt I had to hold onto the unforgiveness in order to punish him. In reality, I was punishing myself and those around me since my demeanor was clouded with unhappiness. It was when I tried to pray and could not find clarity that I opened my heart and cried out to God to help me. My loving Father did and spoke the revelation about forgiveness that changed my life and the dynamics of my family.

I know that God placed people in my life to help me fulfill my destiny and to help me accomplish some of my desires as well. I am sure that the progression in my career was orchestrated by Holy Spirit. I also know that evil appeared alongside the blessing, but it could never stop what God was doing in my life. When I received a promotion to a new position, one of my coworkers was one of the most evil human beings I have encountered. I saw and experienced her deeds but could not believe that she would actually be so vile. She would use her authority to circumvent some of the activities I attempted to implement not because they were unnecessary, but because she sought to make me appear inept. It seemed as if her fingers were in everything, but God always seemed to open another door for me to go through. Consequently, the chief supervisor eventually saw my potential and talent.

I prayed consistently about this situation, but I had much difficulty releasing the unforgiveness toward her. It took a few years after she retired for me to open my heart and allow the Holy Spirit to help me release the anguish and unforgiveness. She is not in my fan club, but I no longer allow her unkind deeds to hold me hostage. Above all, I am most grateful for the faithfulness of God who continued to extend mercy to me during that time of rebellion.

SECTION II

Stories:
MENTORS

feel so blessed, and I am determined to pay it forward. Every opportunity I get to support others and share the love of God, I am willing to do so. I understand the significance of living life to the fullest, seeking the Lord and trusting His Word no matter the circumstances and not depending on an individual to fulfill me.

The love and faith of strong, godly women who loved and supported me and spoke God's truth into my life served as a fountain of life to me. Today, I walk and live in God's life-giving fountain to share with others wherever I find the opportunity.

If you have ever had a strong, loving individual pour into your life, you know what true restoration and support feel like. I shared previously that I grew up with my mother and father in the home. Both loved God and were instrumental in shaping the individual I am today, but in this section, I first want to highlight the great women in my life who spoke the Word as uttered to them by the Holy Spirit. Those utterances scraped me off the floor at times and certainly helped to build a solid foundation in Christ Jesus. I will forever be indebted to the great women who ministered to me and helped me develop my own very intimate and personal relationship with my Lord and Savior Jesus. One has earned her wings in heaven, one is well up in years and still ministering, and the other still speaks into my life, the lives of my children, and everyone God brings across her path.

My mother was a little action-packed, barely five-foot, Spirit-filled woman who literally shot from the hip. This small package bore 12 children from my father, who she married at age 18. She clearly stamped her mark on each of her children.

It wasn't until I gave birth to my first child that I realized the significance of the love of a mother. I recall asking my mom how she managed 12 births—one was enough for me at the time. That is when I began to see my mother as the strong woman she was. I began to see her beyond the person who had always met my basic needs. I began to know her as a kindred woman, friend, and wise spiritual guide.

As I examined my role as mother, I became

unified as an adult to my mother. I turned to her more and more to support me spiritually out of her relationship with God. I knew that she was always available. I knew without doubt that I was loved. I knew that I could count on her. During those times when my life was less than stellar, and it seemed as if the sky was closing in on me no matter what good I gave, my mother was there to comfort, guide, speak God's truths, and stand in the gap with powerful prayer. Knowing I was loved that much helped steer me to know the God of the Bible, her God who was real and ever relevant in her life.

Everyone who knew my mom also knew that she was rather frank. She could never be called tactful. You either accepted it or moved on. But she had such a giving heart. When her health was good, she spent her time visiting the sick in the community and praying for them, sometimes reading the Bible to those at the senior center who could not read.

I recall the day she lost the love of her life— my dad. I stayed with her that night and slept in the bed with her. It was rather unsettling to witness my mom tossing and turning and crying out in her sleep that my father would be missed, she would never love another. The role reversal was uncomfortable, and I felt awkward. What could I possibly say to the strong woman who always strengthened me? What did I have to give to her? I soon recognized my being there was enough, and the bonding was incredible and lasting.

There was a time when I prayed that God would make sure He took my mother and me together. I did not want to ever live on the earth without her. It is amazing how over time God kept us close but required me to grow up emotionally and spiritually. My mother continued to give me the Word of the Lord, but more and more I could share with her revelations that God had given me.

The day my precious little mother left me for good was a Monday in July of 2000. She had spent several months with me in my home after being sick and having surgery. Her request to the Lord was to return home and be able to work in her garden again. Jesus granted her the desire of her heart. She recuperated and returned to reside in her home for a little over a year. When she became ill again, all I saw was faith.

I had visited the hospital every day except the Sunday prior to the Monday she died. I knew her church family and my siblings would be visiting her, and I wanted to allow them to have that uninhibited time with her. I would have her to myself the following day (Monday).

On Monday morning, I was excited to visit with her. I recalled her having said to me on a previous visit, as she lay on her hospital bed looking toward the ceiling, that she had not come here to stay. It was unsettling to me since I expected her to return home again.

I recall that day as if it were yesterday. When I reached the ICU, a nurse pulled me aside and asked if I was the only one to visit. She told me my mother's breathing was labored, and they had to place a device called a bear hugger to assist with breathing; the family should be called in. I explained that family visited the day before, and I had not come. It was difficult to process the information being given, but I recalled later that I had spoken the following to the nurse: "If this is her time, she is ready to go; so be it." In retrospect, I recall how calm and at peace I was. I now understand that even then, the Spirit of God was with me and preparing me for what I call Mom's "great departure."

I walked into her room, greeted her, and kissed her. She seemed glad to see me and gave me a smile. I sat my purse on the table at the foot of her bed and removed her sleep cap in preparation to comb her hair. While talking to her and not hearing any verbal responses, I recall inquiring that she was not talking today. She gave me another smile with a look in her eyes that told me she knew something I did not know. The look was so intriguing. I turned and dropped the sleep cap in my purse and began singing to her as I moved toward the head of her bed to comb her hair. Suddenly, the monitors started beeping wildly. A team came rushing in and escorted me out. On my way downstairs, I heard "code blue" announced. I thought it might be my mom but chose not to believe it to be true. Later after mentally processing the previous 20 minutes, it was clear my sweet mother had waited for me. She knew I had to see her in order to release her. I am forever grateful.

When it was evident that my precious mother was now gone, I started feeling the shock. After making the appropriate contacts, I went to my mother's house. It was so empty. There were many times I spent the night at her house after visiting her in the hospital, and her essence/spirit of life was always evident. On this day, the house was just a building, void of her. It was then that I truly accepted that she was gone.

My mother walked and talked with her God, spirit-to-spirit. I had developed my own relationship with her God, who became my God and friend. I found myself in a relationship as biblically stated: "True worshipers will worship the Father in spirit [from the heart, the inner self] and in truth" (John 4:24 AMP). The day my mother passed, I called my husband, who was attending a funeral in his old community, to share the sad news. He drove to my mother's house to meet me and wait with me as I handled arrangements. We closed up the house and drove home in separate vehicles.

While driving my vehicle behind my husband on our way home that night, I began talking to my friend, Jesus/God. I recall having said to Him that I loved my mother and would miss her so. In the next breath I asked Him to help me no matter what it cost me not to be left behind. I, too, wanted to make it to heaven. Instantly, I heard ever so clearly the following statement in my inner being. "She made it, now it is up to you to make it." I made a vow that evening to serve God with my whole heart. It is a daily love relationship that I would not change for any reason. (So, special thanks to the little woman who birthed me, loved me, chastised me, nurtured me, listened to me and gave me Jesus/God even on the days I wasn't quite sure I wanted or needed Him.)

I also want to share a little about my mother's minister friend who is highly gifted spiritually. She is another prayer warrior. Oftentimes, she would shut in or close herself off from family and friends for a time to fast and pray, spending time in the presence of God for direction and guidance. I have such respect for her and her spiritual gifts. So many times, she spoke words of encouragement and prophetic sayings to me which have come to fruition, some within a short period and others over time. Some of the sayings were life-altering and full of much-needed saving grace. As the Word of God reads, "Nevertheless, do not let this one fact escape your notice, beloved, that with the Lord one day is like a thousand years, and a thousand years is like one day" (II Peter 3:8 AMP). Only mankind is limited by time and space.

Romans 11:29 (AMP) states that "the gifts and the calling of God are irrevocable." God gives gifts to whomever He will. I Corinthians 12:28 defines the ministry gifts.

My bestie/best friend/sister, Vee, is extremely gifted spiritually. If I had to use only one word to describe her, I would say selfless. I have never met an individual as gifted as she is and as giving of herself and God's gifts. She truly is the epitome of what the Scripture says Christians should be.

I cannot count the numerous times I have leaned on her and cried on her shoulder, in person and via phone. The truth/wisdom of God spoken in my life, even when I refused to listen, has been a game changer for me. When ministering, she ministers as God's minister to everyone. The recipient of the ministry never impacts God's wisdom. It comes directly according to what is needed in the manner the Spirit of God deems. She is always careful not to inject her thoughts, and is quick to tell you that she can only share what God gives to her. Anything beyond that is not God.

It is interesting to note that I used to dread being out in public with my bestie. Why? I love her and adore her. But it was as if she had a radar. We could be eating in a restaurant, and she would say, "The couple behind this section is … I am going to minister to them." I recall being in the airport when she saw a child and went over to talk with the mother and child. While doing so, she was also praying for the child because she discerned that the child had a severe medical issue. It did not matter where we were, there was always ministry. Finally, I accepted it after recalling that she was very sensitive and caring as a child. We had the basic material possessions as children but not much else. My bestie would take her clothes to school and give them to children who had far less than we did. She talked about what she saw, and understood some things about people that a child or even an adult would not normally know. She is comfortable with herself and the ability to discern what is and oftentimes what is to come.

She chooses to utilize God's gifts in her for the betterment of others as led by God.

A few years ago, while traveling by automobile, we passed an accident. She began to cry profusely which I did not understand. When she gained her composure, she told me that she felt the injured person's pain and anguish. It grieved her heart so that she had to express it. I recall being in awe. Many years later, I am still in awe of her and the magnitude of her gifts, but ever so appreciative to know her, love her, and be a recipient of the gifts as the Spirit of God ministers.

My heart overflows with love for all of my siblings, but my bestie is the one who walks spirit-to-spirit with me. She is the one who has sacrificed so much to keep me afloat spiritually when I wanted to jump ship and throw in the towel. She picked up where my mother left off but with far more intensity, especially since some of the issues faced could have easily led to my demise without divine intervention. I praise God for His love for me, not because I am so special, for He loves all of His creation. Thank you, Jesus, for my bestie and allowing me to experience you through her gifts and love for you. Thank you, Jesus, for this special gift.

I could not write about my life without also sharing about my father, who was a driving force in my life. He was the spiritual leading force in our family. I adored him, and he was well-liked by almost everyone who met him.

My father was a wonderful Christian man who loved his wife, children, and community. He was well thought of by others and led by example. While dad did not have lots of academics under his belt because he left school as a youngster to help support his family after his own dad died, he was innovative with lots of wisdom. Education was important to him, and he stressed to his children the importance of taking advantage of educational opportunities.

My father prayed with us, took us to church, and taught us Christian values and a good work ethic. He owned a farm and made his living via farming. During my childhood, my father would work with his brother in another part of the state during the time between planting and harvesting. The extra money helped greatly to enhance our provisions.

When I was in the 10th grade, my father had several heart attacks which impaired his health to the extent that he could no longer work. I recall a vivid memory of coming home from school and seeing my father lying on our brown couch not feeling well and most times in pain. I would often hear him say, "Thank you Jesus" over and over. It did not compute. He was in pain yet thanking Jesus. It would be many years before I really understood thanksgiving in the midst of difficult circumstances.

When I graduated from college, my father could not attend due to failing health. I knew he was praying for me and wishing the best for me. After graduation, I visited him as often as possible. I relive our last conversation often. He had suffered a stroke and was recuperating well but had a little slurred speech. I had to listen intently to understand what he was saying. During our last visit what he spoke to me was the flame that ignited my heart to begin my search to truly get to know and serve God. Dad called my name clearly and spoke the following: "Joyce, whatever you do, don't forget to serve the Lord." I promised him I would be obedient, and I kept my promise.

My precious father died in July of 1974. I cannot describe the loss of a parent. His death changed the dynamics of our family because we no longer had the head or compass. Yet, we knew his life and testimony of his relationship with God. He had taught us well, and we would individually go on to develop and/or grow our own relationships with God as we made our way in the world.

SECTION II

Lesson:
GETTING TO KNOW JESUS FOR MYSELF

Every Sunday morning, our father led the family in prayer before breakfast and church. It was not a blessing over the food but a spirit-led prayer of worship and thanksgiving to God. Whoever visited with us during that time was expected to join us in prayer, because our parents revered God above all. Their expectation was that their children would follow the biblical teachings taught in the home. Of course, there comes a time when children reach adulthood and must choose their path, but my choosing the best path would take some time.

I have attended church all of my life. As a child I attended the local Methodist church in the community with my family for almost 20 years until a Spirit-filled minister came to the area. Healings and deliverance were witnessed that revolutionized my parents' faith and view of the believer's relationship with Jesus Christ. During that time, I was young and knew everything, or so I thought. Besides, it felt too atypical to me, and I wanted none of it.

Prior to my parents having attended their first Pentecostal service, it was well known and accepted that our parents loved God and were Christians in good standing in the community. They were blessed with special spiritual gifts that became the norm in our household. We experienced our parents exercising their faith by praying, talking with God and about God, and believing His Word. Their love relationship with God was evident.

When my mother shared something with us that she discerned by the Spirit of God, we believed it with the expectation of seeing it come to pass. I cannot recall anything that we did not see come to pass. The spiritual gifts were passed on through the lineage. Several of the siblings have some form of spiritual gift. I was not sure if I had been so blessed, but it would be years later before I discovered that God had special plans for me also. The spiritual gifts in my life came to the forefront over time as I learned to walk with God and believed biblical truths. You see, as the assumed smart, professional one, everything in my world had to be tangible and fact-related. My analytical mind refused to accept a God I could not see, feel, or taste. From college days until I accepted my parents' God, I lived by what I knew and could see. I attended church because I was raised in the church. Like so many people I was reasonably fair and pretty good to others. I thought of myself as a good person, but this good person was miserable inside.

While visiting with my mom and sister, who resided with my mom at the time while her spouse was overseas, I felt uneasy at witnessing their joy and adoration while discussing the goodness of God and their love for Him. The discussion about talking with God and hearing His voice made no sense to me. But after some time, I became intrigued and wanted to know how one hears from God. How did one know when God was speaking?

During college breaks when I visited at home, I could not negate the change in the atmosphere of our home, positive change in the family. I would describe it as shared in Scripture: the peace that surpasses all understanding. Though still apprehensive, I was yet curious and wanted to believe this new-found attitude would pass. Well, it did not. I soon became more interested, making allusive inquiries from time to time about what they believed. It wasn't long before the sheer loneliness and fears about the future and world issues prompted me to seek after that joy and peace that my parents and sister exhibited.

I always had a sense of God and held the Christian principles to heart. After my first child was born, I felt the desire to find a church for my family. I visited many churches but was unsure of where I should worship. It was after I had an encounter with the Holy Spirit in my home and had accepted Jesus in my heart as my Lord and Savior that I could say for sure that Jesus was real and heart-changing. I immediately felt the change deep in my being, and I knew without a doubt that there had been a change, although I could not explain it. Shortly after this time, Holy Spirit drew me to a church where we could worship and learn God's word.

After this encounter, I fell in love, and I fell hard. My love relationship became better and better over the years, but initially, I was uncertain of a personal communion with the Lord. Reading the Bible and spending time in prayer was what I knew and felt most comfortable doing. I wasn't too interested in moving beyond that.

I truly believed that God spoke to some people in this modern age. In the 1980's, my pastor shared from the pulpit that God did not speak to man. Having heard my pastor, and after having read and watched programs about the supernatural, it just seemed illogical and impossible that I could have such a connection. I was uneasy and wondered if or when the Great I AM would speak to insignificant me. Was it possible? I continued to be curious about my mom and sister's relationship with God. Was it possible to hear the voice of God? Like most of mankind, I could not conceive that some force of power I could not see, yet had been taught to believe in since birth, could or would take time to listen and respond to me. I thought of my parents and my sister as unique individuals. I trusted that they had a divine connection.

I am not all-wise; I can only share what I have truly experienced. The first time I knew that I had heard from God, it happened as follows: I was in my early thirties sitting in church listening to a sermon. The pastor came down from the pulpit and walked past me down the aisle very engaged in teaching his message.

When he turned around on his way back to the pulpit, this calm voice inside my being spoke a comment that had not crossed my mind and did not come from me. I heard a gentle voice clearly state, "I am going to use the least ones." I recall saying to myself, "Wow!" Nevertheless, like Mary, after the angel had visited her and gave the message about the conception of the

Savior, I hid the words in my heart and played them over and over. I did not understand the message then but knew I had received something divine.

Fast-forward years later when I was inundated with teenage woes from my children, personal health issues and more, and life seemed to be overwhelming. My friends and family were great listening ears and always willing to include me in their prayers, but they could not resolve my issues. I turned to Jesus, to get direction and answers. He is "a very present help in trouble" (Psalm 46:1).

I learned easily that I could share anything and everything with my Lord. He was never too busy. No action or thought ever surprised Him. He was not always pleased with my behavior, but His love was constant. His correction and forgiveness as well as His wisdom and revelations were always awe-inspiring. When the songwriter wrote, "I love you Lord; He heard my cry," he had to have walked through some dark places and surfaced in the light. (Jesus is the light of the world.)

Even with the pressures of dealing with life's issues, I had to begin to live what I believed. If I trusted and believed the Word of God, I had to stand on the Word and live the Word believing that all things would work together for my good. Therefore, I began journaling, referencing my communications with God. This served as a huge encouragement since I had documented reminders of how God moved in my life.

My prayer life became paramount. I prayed and talked with the Lord on the way to and from work daily. I prayed periodically throughout the day. In the midst of my prayers, I began to develop a heart of thankfulness and gratefulness. It became easier for me to begin my day with thanksgiving than with complaints and requests. It was then that I began to experience the lifting of the cloud that seemed to overshadow me. I continued to thank the Lord for working my situation out for my good because I truly believed He would come to my rescue. I believed Him to be the faithful God of the Bible who does not change.

I discovered that God's answers always come, but they may not come in our expected timeline or format. The process leading to the solution almost always teaches a lesson or purpose. If we don't learn the lesson, we are more than likely to sojourn again and again in the desert until we do. I have experienced many episodes in the desert.

SECTION III

Stories:
MARRIAGE AND FAMILY

I have shared that fantasy was a major part of my life. Within this fantasy world, I thought many times about the man I would marry, and how he would love and adore me the way my father adored my mother. Most individuals fall in love with the best intentions. Usually, the woman has the fantasy about the wonderful family life with her husband and children living happily ever after. What is usually missing is the fact that there are two different individuals in the mix, often from different backgrounds and varied experiences. The mix does not always produce the desired outcome, at least not initially.

While I believe the attitude of the heart drives everything, no human being can change the heart. Only the creator of mankind can change a heart. That change can only happen if the individual is willing to allow change, because

God gave mankind free will. If we seek Him, we can find Him. It took a while and numerous circumstances for me to realize my need for a personal heart change because I was just seeking God for change in my circumstances and family, not for me personally.

I had incurred pain and anguish at various stages of my life as most individuals do. It resulted in my becoming a bitter, unhappy woman. I often wondered how I would overcome this state. Of course, I was not aware of the bitterness until the Holy Spirit pointed it out to me. I would not have believed it otherwise. As a mother with young children, it was imperative that they experience the best of me.

I knew enough truth to know that I had to be willing to let go of my right to hold onto the bitterness which was accompanied by lots of unforgiveness. It did not happen overnight, but experiencing Jesus day by day helped me to realize that forgiveness is liberating. I believe Scripture, and Scripture states that we must forgive and love our brethren since Christ forgave and continues to forgive us.

Marriage interactions provide the opportunity to practice forgiveness again and again. I wish I could share that I was good at doing so, but like most individuals, I had some breezy days and many more pressing-through days.

Consequently, I learned that we cannot be responsible for the behavior of others, just our own behavior.

Spouses know the best of us and the worst of us. They know the pressure points and can activate them at will. A partner who is willing to do the work necessary to mature in the marriage and work together as a couple will seek to handle issues and disagreements in the best possible manner that is neither injurious to the partner nor the marriage.

The best definition of love and how love should be defined in marriage and any other relationship is provided in Scripture. It states that, "Love endures with patience and serenity, love is kind and thoughtful, and is not jealous or envious; love does not brag and is not proud or arrogant. It is not rude; it is not self-seeking, it is not provoked [nor overly sensitive and easily angered]; it does not take into account a wrong endured" (1 Corinthians 13:4-5 AMP).

When we got married, I was a 21-year-old who gave her heart away to a young man from a neighboring community. Both of us were raised in Christian homes but with very different dynamics. I had dated minimally in high school and college, but I had never been in love. I was selective in seeking a partner. I had hoped for one who embodied the attributes modeled by my father. Christian principles and life-long, forever-after commitments were a must. Like most little girls who played with dolls and fantasized about getting married and living happily ever after, I wanted my prince charming, children, and a lovely life. Having grown up in a two-parent, stable home environment, I wanted and expected the same.

I recall that I first met my husband one Sunday afternoon when we were introduced by a girl who lived down the road from me. There was no immediate interest, no sparks. We met again a few years later, on a double date. Many phone conversations later, we became an item, but I was a high school senior who went off to college. My beau, who was attending the community college at the time, was drafted and went off to serve our country.

The saying that distance makes the heart grow fonder seemed to work in our situation. We shared our heart through countless letters, and a few years later when my sweetheart came home, we eloped and got married. I was a college senior, so we kept our marriage a secret until Christmas vacation when we told our families. After graduation in May of the next year, I moved back home excited about being a wife and new college graduate. Unfortunately, the glamorous life I had imagined was far from my reality. Settling in as a young wife and meshing personalities proved to be difficult. Having to reside in the very place I had longed to escape added insult to injury.

Two years later, we welcomed our first child, a daughter. She was the best gift I had ever received, next to the birth of our son a little more than four years later. I loved being a mother. It was as if I was put on earth for motherhood. I relished every growth stage, every new tooth, new word, and more. I poured my life into my children even though I worked outside the home. I made sure that they were involved in extracurricular activities and always had support for school events.

My husband was working shifts at the time, and when our schedules connected, he gave some time to the children, but our relationship began to dissolve. We ate together as a family when possible, and continued to take yearly family vacations, but we had minimal conversation and spent most of our time apart doing other things. We did not attend church as a family; it was just me and the children. He and I did not hang out with other adults. So, before we realized it, our children were teens, and we were strangers.

I had always turned to God during the tough times in my life, and this time was no different.

I prayed for cohesiveness in my family and renewal in my marriage. However, things were to get far worse long before there was improvement. There was detachment, separation, and alienation on and off for years. I learned to cope by embracing the good days and avoiding interaction during the other. Had I not had the love of my children and mom, I don't know if I would have remained in the marriage.

There came a time when I did not want to make an effort to keep the marriage together. I felt as if I was married to a stranger, and I wanted things to be over so I could have mental stability and peace. I had reached my limit and wanted out. I did not want to date or party, I just wanted normalcy.

It seemed my prayers had been in vain, and I began to feel that God had abandoned me, but what I did not know during that time was that God had a plan for our lives. I was under a heavy blanket of oppression and did not know how to escape. Nevertheless, I would eventually fight my way out of the darkness and cry out to God for help.

The more I turned to God, the more healing came to my heart. I learned that God is never without a plan even if we can't see it. He knows the end from the beginning and delights in relationship with His creation. So, the more I prayed, the more I changed, even though it seemed as if my situation got worse. The softening of my heart allowed me to receive revelation from God that continues to impact my family even in the present day.

God taught me about the power of forgiveness, strength to overcome, faith, and love. I learned, after many years of refusing to allow God in, that some of us are destined to walk a walk that mortally impacts the lives of others. We don't usually choose the role; God chooses it for us. The call is dropped in our Spirit. Some run from it and never fulfill it. Others find themselves in war-torn countries sharing the gospel, in remote, impoverished areas sharing God's love, in families seemingly being handed a raw deal, or without family and feeling desolate and alone. Regardless of the situation, God is faithful, and we can trust Him to help us fulfill our assigned call (see Psalm 37:3).

How does God complete His work in the earth? After the cross and a brief time on the earth, Scripture tells us Jesus returned to heaven having left the hope that He would return to us. He sent the Holy Spirit to guide, teach, and make intercession for believers of the gospel. The Spirit of God works in and through the people of God who have willing hearts (see John 14:23-26).

The Spirit of God has ministered to me as far back as I can remember, through my parents, family, minister friends, pastors, casual friends, and finally one-on-one to me when I really knew without a doubt that it was God. Relationship develops a familiarity that makes it easy to recognize your friend. I learned to walk in relationship with my friend, Jesus. Developing a love relationship has been a life saver for me, my family, and all those to whom I have had the liberty of sharing the love of Jesus.

The greatest testimony is in my home, where I have seen and continue to see the miracle-working power of God. I have come to understand that we are saved by acknowledging and accepting Jesus in our heart as Lord and Savior. What many believers don't know is that the experience continues throughout our lives. Once we willingly receive Christ, we continue to be exposed to the best and worst of life. Thus, if we allow the Spirit of God to operate as designed, we continue to change degree by degree to reflect the likeness of Christ.

Humanity is full of error. Scripture tells us that the heart is wicked (see Jeremiah 17:9). So even with the best intentions, the sin nature of humanity is alien to the things of God. When my heart began to be transformed by the washing of the Word of God, and filled with the love of God, I became equipped with a love that looks beyond the circumstance and person to hear and obey the very one who gave His all for me and humanity. It is a daily walk, a daily seeking of the will of God and allowing Him to transform the heart. I am learning to love the unlovable and extend mercy where mercy has not been given because that is what Jesus does for me every day of my life. It is the power of the cross that makes the impossible possible and extends forgiveness to undeserving humanity (see Isaiah 53).

God was renewing and building me up while my marriage was in shambles. During that time, my sweet mother became seriously ill, requiring that I spend more time with her. My children were older teens at the time and pretty much unsupervised and taking advantage of the opportunity. I did not know how much more I could bear. It is the nature of a good parent to want the very best for their children. A mother's heart hurts tremendously when her children's lives are out of order. We want the very best for them and will do almost anything necessary to ensure they have life's best. Of course, I wanted them to have the material things, but above all, I wanted them to follow the teachings of their youth and become good Christian adults.

Trusting God in such circumstances is a

blind faith walk. What choice is there? I could have chosen the vices others used to cope with difficulties, but when the vices wear off, the problems are still present. I realized that I needed help, but I also remembered the scripture, "Trust in the Lord with all thine heart; and lean not unto thine own understanding. In all thy ways acknowledge him, and he shall direct thy paths" (Proverbs 3:5-6).

I cast my cares on the Lord by praying and reading the Scriptures constantly. I prayed all the way to work in the mornings during my 30-minute drive. It became easy, and I looked forward to my time with the Lord. I really learned to walk and talk with God during that trying time. We conversed freely. He made promises to me about my children which I hid in my heart and fought to hold onto as I observed their steady march into the glitz and superficial glamour of the world.

"Weeping may endure for a night, but joy comes in the morning" (Psalm 30:5 NKJV). I was reminded of that scripture many times over the years as I prayed relentlessly for my children to return to Christ and for my husband to serve God, and for myself as I glimpsed snapshots of areas of my own heart that needed to be transformed.

The promises of God are "Yes" and "Amen"

(see II Corinthians 1:20 NKJV). God came through as promised. Today, both of my children are serving God as He promised me they would. They continue to thank me for standing in faith during those trying times in their lives. They have expressed gratitude for my showing them the love of Jesus while not condoning their error. I am forever grateful to the all-wise, faithful Savior.

SECTION III

Lesson:
A FEW OF GOD'S PROMISES TO ME AND INDISPUTABLE MIRACLES

The Bible is full of promises for those who believe. It covers some of every experience known to mankind. The Word is God-breathed. The Word also states that God is the same today as He was in the biblical days and will continue to be so (Hebrews 13:8 AMP). So, as God walked and talked with mankind as He chose, He also healed, delivered, raised from the dead, gave glimpses of the future, and more.

Promise: "Children Will Serve God"

My daughter did well in school, went off to college for a year, and returned home to work and continue college at home while also attending Bible school.

Along the way, she made some decisions that would alter her Christian walk. She turned her back on Jesus and sought a lifestyle that was contrary to what she had been taught.

My son was difficult to conceive. I had a twin pregnancy, but lost one of the babies early in the pregnancy, which grieved my heart. I knew my remaining baby would be fine because the Holy Spirit allowed me to see him in a vision or dream. When he was born, he did look exactly like the infant in my vision. He was healthy and normal, and I knew that retaining a baby in the womb in the early stages after losing one was a miracle.

My son was academically gifted and did very well in school. The expectation after high school was college and more. However, once he got a taste of the world, it seemed to invade his life. He forgot his Christian values and spent several years apart from God.

It was devastating to me. I felt that if my life did not come together in my home, work, and other, I could at least take joy in the fact that my children were doing well. It seemed as if my world was crumbling around me. I could not fix it no matter how much I tried. My solution was to turn to God. I reminded Him of His promise, and stood on that promise until I saw it come to fruition.

My daughter renewed her relationship with Jesus after much ministry from family and

Christian friends. The foundation was already there, so Holy Spirit was welcomed to reconnect. Today, she is married and serving Jesus with her husband and children.

The change came much later for my son, after God moved on his heart to return home to be closer to family. He found a good job but had not found his way back in relationship with God. However, he had a life-altering experience that brought about situations that would present a domino effect in his life.

My son tore his ACL during a pickup basketball game and had to have surgery. He had never had surgery of any kind. A few days after his surgical procedure, we returned to the doctor for a post-op visit.

We stopped at the bank after the visit to cash his paycheck. While waiting on the teller to assist us in the drive-through, I engaged him in conversation. I had no idea that my conversation would jumpstart a life change for him, nor did I realize that the Holy Spirit was speaking until later. Holy Spirit spoke the following through me:

You are a smart young man with a college degree under your belt. What are your friends doing with their lives? You cannot continue to party forever. The Word says iron sharpens iron. What are you giving to your friends? Either you are pulling them up or they are pulling you down. Are you going to be old men someday, still partying and accomplishing nothing with your lives?

While it may have seemed like a lifetime before the teller came to the window, it was a brief time. Yet it was life-changing because a few days later, my son shared with me that what had been spoken to him in the car had stirred up something that he could not dismiss. It caused him to begin reading the Word and praying. He could open his heart with the desire to fellowship with God. Out of that came deliverance, renewal, spiritual growth, and a determination to serve God as never before.

I watched this young man become serious about his walk with the Lord. The partying ceased. His choice of friends changed, and he began praying for his mate. Although there were young ladies who sought after him, he made vows to God and refused to change his standard of living as directed by Holy Spirit. He is waiting for his mate who will serve God with him.

"Spouse Will Attend Church With Family"

Approximately 20-plus years after receiving

this prophecy, my husband decided to attend church with me, He had attended church with his father and brothers about 35 minutes away from our home in prior years. It was his childhood home church. He was hostile and adamant against attending church with his wife and children. In fact, he was verbally aggressive and unkind about the church I attended with the children, although we had been in membership for over 10 years. At best, it was a difficult home environment since now we could add arguing about churches to our long laundry list.

I was happy that my husband finally decided to attend church, but weary that he dismissed his immediate family to go elsewhere. I became even sadder when after attending church, there was no change of heart in the way he responded and handled matters in our home. It seemed like things got worse. Of course, the day came when he insisted we leave our church and attend church with him. I knew God had given me a promise.

Was this it? It did not feel right in my spirit, although it sounded like the right action to take.

Well, since I learned to pray about situations before taking a leap, I did just that. Holy Spirit told me this was not in God's plan for us.

Needless to say, I heard a lot of religious rhetoric about the duties of the Christian wife, all of it quoted incorrectly.

Except we agree, how could we walk together? If there was ever a time to walk by faith and not by sight as stated in the Scriptures, that was the time.

The next few years were dark. My husband became more and more religious, cold, detached, and sarcastic, pointing out every error regardless of how small. The favorite phrase used was, "You say you are a Christian!"

God uses the foolish things to confound the wise. In 2009 on my birthday, I fell out of the attic of my old house and broke my leg and crushed my knee. I had to have surgery and endured a long recovery and rehabilitation. My husband stepped in and cared for me. The support he gave was astounding and welcomed, since I was in a wheelchair.

At that time Holy Spirit had moved me to another ministry but not to my husband's home church. While recuperating, I expressed a desire to attend church, and he agreed to take me. After a few visits, he joined and began hearing and learning God's truths. We continued to worship together, and later our adult children became active in the ministry.

God did not cause my accident. The evil one attempted to take my life, but my sweet Jesus saved me and ministered to my husband who softened his heart to care for me. In the process, he was available to receive when Holy Spirit also knocked on his heart. Who would have guessed a near-tragedy would have generated a blessing and fulfilled God's promise? Scripture describes this occurrence in Romans 8:28: "All things work together for good to them that love God, to them who are the called according to his purpose."

"New Job"

After 14 years as a classroom teacher, I sought a new position. After praying about it, I received the promise that I would be appointed to the position I desired. Little did I know that it would take seven years before the promise was fulfilled.

Once I received the promise, I told my peers at work that I would be leaving soon. I was excited and bubbling over knowing that the following year I would be working in my new position. Well as you might suspect, it did not happen the way I had planned.

I made my supervisor aware that I wanted to transfer when a position became available. Wouldn't you know it, at the end of that school year, the very position I longed for became available. I just knew it was mine.

I was almost salivating over it. During that time, seven of my peers received transfers to positions they desired, and I did not understand why I had not heard any information about my position.

The new school year began, and after having announced to almost everyone that I would not be returning to the school, I was devastated by the end of the summer vacation since I had heard nothing about my transfer. I did not think I could return, but after some great ministry, I picked myself up, repented for the pride and arrogance, and returned to my old position to have the best year ever. I knew that my time would come when God thought I was ready.

Close to the end of the school year, exactly seven years later, my supervisor came to see me and spoke the following: "I recall that you wrote me a letter requesting a move to a new position. Well, I need to know if you are still interested."

I almost fainted because Holy Spirit had told me not to apply for another position. He would let me know when it was time to move. So, of course, I was petrified. I could not respond without quickly consulting Holy Spirit. He said, "Listen, this job is for you."

So, I responded that I was still interested, and my supervisor told me about a sought-after position at the high school that many others wanted. She said specifically that she wanted me to have that position. The new job proved to be a gateway to bigger and better. (Look at God!)

"New Home"

My husband and I were blessed to build a nice home when I was 26 years old; our daughter was 24 months old. I loved my new home and did my best to make it comfortable for my family. I assumed my husband and I would grow old in that house. It held many memories.

Our son was born to us almost five years later. We raised our children there and remained in this residence for over 30 years. There were lots of wonderful memories of the children and our young married relationship, and some not-so-good memories of the dark days.

I often felt in my spirit that it would be great to move and start over in a fresh environment. Later, I learned that we needed to begin to deal with our issues according to God's will in order to receive the desires of our heart that God desired to give us. He is merciful to us even when we are not pleasing to Him.

In 1994, I made my request for a new home

while in prayer. I heard Holy Spirit tell me I could have it. I had no idea of what, how, or when. I simply stored the promise and kept striving to be obedient and repenting when I missed it. In 2014, 20 years later, we moved into our new home that we helped design. It all seemed like a dream, but God is faithful and cares about everything that concerns us, regardless of how large or small. The key is that it must be in His will for us, and we can only know His will about any situation if we seek Him to discover it.

"Strengthening of Marriage"

I have experienced sweetness and kindness and relationship that only the Creator of the universe could bring to pass. The odds were surely against my marriage making it, but much prayer and ongoing supplication helped to birth a relationship filled with agape love. Only God can make something worthwhile out of shambles. I praise God for continuing to fulfill His promises.

Please see more about this relationship in Section IV: Struggle.

"Protection"

The Word of God says that the enemy comes to steal, kill and destroy. The world may count situations in life as mere circumstances, but I have learned to be aware of evil in the world. I know my God is superior to anything the evil one attempts. Thus, it is important that believers live in the world but not be of the world, for the evil one goes to and fro "seeking whom he may devour" (I Peter 5:8).

Since God gave man dominion over the earth and free will, man has free choice to serve God or not. However, without the protection of the living God, and His Spiritual arsenal, believers would be wide open to the evils of the enemy. Jesus provides hope, salvation, guidance, and Divine protection. We just have to accept the Savior and what He has to offer: life more abundantly while on the earth and life eternally thereafter.

I have experienced divine protection as far back as I can recall. In my youth, I was covered by the prayers of my parents and saved from many adverse situations. I did not understand then the significance of God and personal relationship. I can recall many incidents, some of which I am now sharing with you:

1. While on vacation with my family, I was driving home with my spouse and our children who were asleep in the backseat. It began to rain with a torrential downpour which eroded conditions where I could barely see the highway. I slowed down trying

to find a place to pull over safely. Although I could barely see through the heavy sheets of rain, I did glimpse some cars that were parked on the side of the highway. I pulled over at the first clear space.

While waiting for the rain to clear, I noticed in my rearview mirror a car speeding toward the rear of my vehicle. Fearing I would be hit from the rear, I made a quick attempt to start my car to move out of the way but was not fast enough. Suddenly, the speeding car stopped short of my vehicle as its hood flew open.

I had no idea that during that time, my mother's dear evangelist friend was visiting with her. During their visit, she told my mother that the enemy was attempting to destroy me, but God would protect me. Praise be to God who sees all, knows all, and protects His children.

When the rain subsided, my husband and I changed positions, so he could drive. We noticed several wrecked cars ahead of us and a few well behind us. The car that had sped toward my vehicle earlier was less than two feet from my rear bumper. Immediately, I recognized that God had granted a miracle to us. I was so grateful that the angel of the Lord had stopped that speeding bullet because had the car hit us, we would probably have suffered serious injury.

2. The next incident was mentioned earlier—my fall from the attic. I am sharing the details because it is important to share how the miracles unfolded on that special day.

We had resided in that home for over 30 years, and I had accessed the pull-down attic far more times than I can recall. However, on this Veteran's Day in 2009, which was also my birthday, I decided to take down Christmas decorations and store them on the first level for easy access when it was time to decorate.

I went up the steps and took down two bags. On my second trip, I was standing on the stairs with my upper body in the attic. I have no recall of what happened next. I just know that I fell, landing on my left foot. I heard a crunch and experienced pain that was indescribable.

The pain was excruciating, so much so that I almost fainted. I was obviously in shock, but had I passed out, it would have been at least six hours before someone found me.

Within seconds, I literally felt the light touch of someone. It felt as if I had been placed in a more comfortable position. At that point,

I became calm and rational, realizing that I had experienced contact with a supernatural being that I believed to be my Guardian Angel, especially since I was at home alone.

I pulled myself down the hallway toward the den, using my whole right side to propel myself, until I reached the chair that contained my purse and phone so I could call my husband. Thankfully, I had not taken my purse to my bedroom as usual.

Thank God once again for His ministering angels who sustained me in the midst of adversity. Others may say they should have prevented my falling. I believe I lived because they intervened; I learned shortly thereafter that someone else had suffered a similar fall and had broken their neck. Although I will have the surgical scar for a lifetime, it is a reminder to me of God's mercy.

"Healing and Restoration"

I received a medical diagnosis almost 15 years ago that was mind-boggling. No one in my family had suffered with this condition, and I was shaken with fear by information spoken to me by the medical community. I had great physicians who worked with me to create the finest treatment, but the long-term prognosis was not promising.

As with all other situations in my life, I turned to the one who created me. I needed to hear what my Jesus had to say about the situation. I received the Word of the Lord from the Throne Room. I was told that certain things spoken would not come to pass, and I was encouraged to pray, serve Him, and do my part. He would do the rest. So, I got involved in my medical treatment, asking questions and following instructions but seeking godly wisdom about each process.

While exuberant over the Word from God, I soon realized that I had to live day by day following the medical regime prescribed currently while holding onto the promise. Even when matters seemed dire, Holy Spirit intervened. I have known many with the diagnosis who are no longer alive, but I am still here, functioning well and holding God's promises in my heart.

Yes, there are times when I get lost in my mind because of words spoken or minor symptoms, but the mercy of God has superseded all that I could ever hope or imagine. Consequently, my faith level has skyrocketed to higher levels, and every day I am walking and living out my healing and deliverance as my Lord has instructed me to do.

I believe the Bible in its entirety. It clearly states that God is "the same yesterday, and today, and forever" (Hebrews 13:8). Therefore, I expect God to move in my life. I realize that He moves according to His plans and purposes. So, if I live, I live for Jesus. If I die, I die in Jesus to gain the greatest life. Yet while I reside on the earth, I desire to prosper and live in health as my soul prospers. It is my right and every other believer's right of access made available through the Cross at Calvary. (Today, I defy medical predictions because God has spoken.)

God has plans for all of his children. Often-times, we have to be in a quiet place, shutting out the conflicting voices in our being to rest and hear Holy Spirit. I hear best in quiet alone times, but I also hear infrequently otherwise.

While at a major medical center and under-going a serious test, I was stressed and fearful, especially since I had to be strapped down to undergo the 20-minute test. I prayed fervently in order to rest in Jesus since it felt like my heart would beat out of my chest. A few minutes into the process, Holy Spirit began speaking to me.

He said, "Daughter, give my love away!" Such love and peace flooded my being. I became calm instantly and began talking to my Lord. Those words changed my Christian walk forever. Now, I seek to share His love consistently in some way whether it is a smile or tangible act.

SECTION IV

Stories:
STRUGGLE

Year after year I wondered, prayed, and cried out to God countless times about why I seemed to continue to sojourn in the desert even with bouts of relief. My journey, as described in earlier sections, eventually revealed my lack of revelation and understanding.

I had listened to numerous Spirit-filled messages that rightly divided the Word. They inspired me to move forward in Jesus, and it seemed that God had truly issued my release to move forward in peace and soundness, but I kept finding myself stuck and repeating the same cycle.

It was quite some time, years later, before I understood that I was meant to learn something concrete that would revolutionize my world. Either I was too dull to ascertain or just too stubborn to let go of my desire to handle matters my way.

Stubborn is a gentler term. Scripture describes it as stiff-necked and rebellious. Was God listening to my requests? Had I lost favor? I had to get beyond this place of quicksand. Imagine the deeply ingrained disappointment. My thoughts and questions were reverberating loudly in my being: Why me, Lord? Why can't I be free of this journey?

I had reached the point where I no longer wanted to be married, because I did not want to pay the price required of me to have a successful marriage. I loved my husband, but I could not bear the drama that my life had become. I knew Christ; he did not. The more I grew in Christ, the more detached and unkind he became. While I prayed God's best for him, I knew he could not possibly be the man God had chosen for me. We had married prior to my becoming a Christian, and I needed my partner to serve God with me. My heart was dead, and I wanted out.

The thing about being in a valley is that you eventually have to look up. My upward view at times inspired me. So, after a time of questioning Holy Spirit, I found myself in my prayer closet seeking God with my whole heart. Scripture tells us to seek Him, and we will find Him. I sought God fervently, and I found Him.

I was reminded of how painful it was for

Jesus at Gethsemane just before He went to Calvary to bear the sins of the world. Certainly, I am not equating myself with Jesus. My issues, unlike those our Lord faced, dealt mainly with pride, which will destroy you. I had refused to let go and die to self or open my heart fully to God. I was stuck on not allowing my husband, who I viewed as my adversary, to win the battle of wills. What a selfish believer I had become.

Jesus cried out to His Father to receive strength to make it through the deep, dark, heavy ordeal that He had to face. His ordeal was far more heinous than anything anyone has had to face since the beginning of time. He made it possible for me and all other mankind to access liberty in the Spirit. Therefore, having come to the realization that the liberty of Jesus was truly there for me, I had the choice to relent and to initiate God's plan in my heart and subsequently in my home.

God loves us far more than we could ever hope or think. When we think all possible has been done, He shows up with a plan that supersedes anything mere man could ever conjure up. In my case, Holy Spirit had gently pressed me for heart changes over the years. He never forces since man has been given freewill.

I honestly thought I was in a pretty good place spiritually. I could not really see myself, nor did I want to. I now understand that heart changes occur throughout our lives if we allow them to, since Holy Spirit is always drawing us to God. Those who seek to live close to Jesus will find that Holy Spirit will always make Himself accessible.

Incremental heart changes were taking place over the years, but I did not recognize it. The heart has layers of life's issues. The spiritual supporters in my life noticed the changes in me and continued to encourage me. The encouragement kept me pressing forward enough to fight willingly and consistently for myself and others that Holy Spirit put on my heart. The lesson learned is that believers must have encouragers in their lives to support them through the difficult times.

I have always operated from the position that I was submitted to God. I understood submission in marriage as specified in the Bible, but did not feel I could possibly operate with that degree of submission to my spouse. My view of submission here is working cooperatively to accomplish a goal. I was strong-willed and opinionated with a heart full of offense and pride, which would most certainly lead to failure.

My husband had no real understanding of God's instruction about submission in marriage, or what a normal marriage really should look like. He was a good father and a great provider, but he had his own share of difficulties and insecurities that he needed to release to God. Throw in his lack of spiritual knowledge and the imbalance in parental roles experienced in his own life, and you had a recipe that just could not yield a well-balanced marital relationship.

God is faithful, persistent, and consistent in His faithfulness and love for His creation. He cannot move our will because our will is a privilege He grants to humanity. He does provide circumstances to help us adjust our will if we choose to do so. His mercy and blessings overtake the believer where possible, but those little foxes, or areas of self-will and rebellion that we refuse to acknowledge or handle appropriately, or perhaps those hidden areas of the heart we don't know about, often trip us up.

Everyone has those hidden areas, e.g., jealousy and envy, unforgiveness, etc., which could have been generated from any number of life's experiences. We pack them down and move on, not realizing their existence until something triggers an emotion. At that point, we may wonder why we responded in a certain way or felt a certain way. Scripture tells us that man should "pray without ceasing" (I Thess. 5:17). As we become more knowledgeable about God and His requirements for mankind, we should pray that those areas of our heart that are contrary to God's nature be replaced with His love, which covers "a multitude of sins" (I Peter 4:8 NIV).

Holy Spirit gave me revelation about my biblical charge as wife and my requirement to come under the spiritual headship of the position of husband rather than focus on fleshly led ego and insecure man, as required in Scripture, specifically Ephesians 5. Then the revelation became clear to me that my submission was to God, even as I operated in my role as wife. This enlightenment brought freedom, peace, and a greater desire to please God. I could avoid the bondage that the term submission represented to me and still obey God.

The greatest clarity came via the revelation that it was not my job to change my spouse, nor was I appointed as his judge. My responsibility was to seek God, speak truth in love, and represent God's truth in action by hearing God and obeying day by day. This obedience, on my part, opened the door for the Great I AM to move in my lifelong situation where He was hindered previously. It was liberating!

I know it does not happen like that for everyone. God knew the real me. He knew my heart, regardless of how I hid it from others. He knew what was necessary for me to get to where I needed to be in order to live a Spirit-filled life and to fulfill the call of God on my life.

The avenues I came through prepared me to live as nothing else could have. I had no other choice but to learn to walk and live by faith and not by sight. I continue to forge ahead with excitement, thankfulness, and faith that God knows what is best for me. His plans and oversight are far greater than anything I could have manufactured.

My advice to believers is to seek revelation through reading God's Word. Many people have their own interpretation of Scriptures, but only the author of the written Word knows His intent. He desires that we seek understanding through Scripture, for what we do and how we do it affects lives and souls. Holy Spirit is always willing and ready to teach us if we are willing to submit our hearts to learn.

I know that cutting losses and moving on from a marriage that isn't working is the norm for today's society. Well, I certainly entertained that idea many times over the years. Christians get divorced every day. However, my story is a little different. It does not mean I am better; it simply means that God had a plan for us, and I accepted the hand of mercy extended to me that is available to every believer.

I now understand that souls are often assigned to us. Each person is certainly responsible for the truths made available, what they have learned, as well as how they have lived their lives. But sometimes, believers are given the responsibility to stand in the gap and intercede for others. I learned this personally from Holy Spirit.

I praise God for those who were assigned to pray for me. Their obedience and prayers helped me along life's journey to get to a point in life where I desired God, sought after Him fervently, and found Him. Now, I understand the significance of praying for others, even if it takes years. For one day in the eyes of God is as a thousand years, and "a thousand years as one day" (II Peter 3:8 NKJV).

The prayers of the believers are active, accomplishing God's purpose. Many times, we do not get to see the results of our prayers, because prayer crosses distance and time. That is why we pray in faith, believing that our prayers will come to fruition.

Many years ago, after a heated disagreement with my spouse, I threw my hands up and told Holy Spirit I was finished. My husband did not know God, did not want to know God at the time, and could not understand my desire to live for God. I was desperate and really wanted my family as a unit to serve God. I knew that was the will of God and the answer for my family.

I told God that day that I was sick and tired of the constant bickering and unhappy environment that seemed to prevail in our home. I wanted to raise my children with Christian values and enjoy life, and I felt that I could not take another day of animosity and strife. I was truly finished. Immediately after uttering those words, Holy Spirit spoke strongly to me the following: "Your being 'sick and tired' means that soul goes to hell!"

Sobering and lasting were those words that echoed in my being, that day and every time afterwards, when things became difficult and I felt the urge to throw in the towel. I learned that in the darkest of times, prayer will get you through.

The more I prayed, the closer I grew to God, and more of my selfish behavior began to fade. Now, I have a burden in my spirit that causes me to spend much time in prayer interceding for the lost.

I am determined to see this journey through. I have to live with an intentional perspective even when my flesh screams otherwise. It is often a fight, but I refuse to stand before the Kings of Kings and Lord of Lords at the end of my days not having interceded for souls, and especially for the one soul I knew was assigned to me.

The labor of intercession has ushered in many other souls, some I will never know, but the burden for souls has sprouted in my heart. Today I recognize that life is far less about me, although I have my moments. I am driven and focused on hearing and obeying Holy Spirit day by day.

Another catalyst of major change in my heart and life came as a direct result of a different mandate from Holy Spirit while in prayer one morning many years later. My husband and I had moved into our new home, and I just knew this was the last rough patch. We were moving into the home God promised us 20 years before, the land of milk and honey.

Well, it was far from that. Ten months after our move, my husband had open-heart surgery to repair several closed arteries. This was his first hospitalization and surgery. God brought him through the surgery, and with rehabilitation he would have a long, healthy life.

The real test for me came during his recuperation time at home. I made every effort to follow the physician's orders and reported any concerns to the outpatient nurse who came weekly, but as a patient my husband became someone I simply did not know. He was hostile and refused to follow the explicit instructions of his doctor except for taking his meds and eating properly only because I oversaw the meds and prepared the meals.

The required exercise regimen was dismissed, no matter how much I prodded and begged. The hostility at every juncture became overwhelming for me and brought me to tears on many days. I prayed for strength and endurance because I felt as if I were in a war zone. Nevertheless, a good soldier gets the job done. Praise God, He brought me through another difficult place.

When my husband was released to drive, he was elated at his new freedom. I was happy to see him regaining good health, but he was not the same person. We had become distant. It seemed I was always reminding him of appropriate eating and exercise out of my concern for him. He was determined to eat what he wanted, when he wanted and to simply settle in to his former routine. Our relationship had reached a stalemate.

One special morning in prayer, the message I received from Holy Spirit revolutionized our lives and jumpstarted our marriage to a level greater than ever before. I was given the mandate that we were to begin our day with prayer and end our day with prayer. Well, that was tremendous for a couple who barely spoke during the day. Surprisingly to me, my husband agreed because Holy Spirit had moved on his heart, and he was receptive. Praying together made us more engaged, and we began to look forward to our prayer time together as well as to spending quality time as a couple.

SECTION IV

Lesson:
ETERNAL LIFE IS AVAILABLE TO EVERYONE

My goal here is to share the love of Christ, the power of Christ and the significance and depth of his faithfulness beyond what any of us could imagine. He will go the distance for any of us if we ask. He loves His creation just that much. God is the Father, and Jesus is God's Son, created in God's image. The Holy Spirit is the Spirit of God who is holy. All three members of the Godhead are holy. They operate independently and as one, and are often identified as the Trinity.

Scripture tells us that the Holy Spirit is on the earth serving as an advocate for believers. He was sent to support believers after Jesus died on the cross and left the earth to return to heaven (see John 14:26).

I would be remiss if I did not make you aware that while the essence of our holy God is in the earth to support believers, the evil that we see and experience in the earth is through another spirit that is evil, always does evil, and tries his best to trick us into believing that his way is the right way or that there is no God. Scripture describes him well. He is the devil. As you read Scripture, especially in the New Testament, you will become more aware of his tricks. He cannot make you do anything, but he can influence you to go astray. You have experienced him numerous times in negative thoughts, bad language you felt like using easily, and wrong deeds done without really thinking about them, wondering why afterwards.

1 John 3:8 says "The reason the Son of God appeared was to destroy the devil's work" (NIV). We can always pray God's protection over our minds and bodies. We who belong to Jesus have an advocate; therefore, we are not to fear the evil one but must be aware of evil around us. Strive to avoid what does not bring glory to God.

Visions of the world as we know it today are indeed daunting. Truthfully, the world is very dark, but Jesus is the light, joy, peace, and confidence we need to live life abundantly. We who know the Word have the privilege of seeing the Bible prophesies rapidly being fulfilled. Believers need not fear but should be experiencing an excitement in their Spirit that King Jesus is returning to the earth soon. We cannot be complacent but must be readily working in the harvest reaping whenever and wherever the Holy Spirit leads. Jesus said, "'the harvest truly is plentiful, but the laborers are few. Therefore pray the Lord of the harvest to send out laborers … '" (Matthew 9:37-38 NKJV). Believers are the much-needed laborers referenced.

So, be encouraged. Know today that Jesus loves you, no matter what has happened in your life, whether it happened to you or you committed the unthinkable. The horrors endured at the Cross by Jesus, who was the only one qualified to pay the price for the sins of all mankind, took place so we could live and have life more abundantly. God loves sinners and believers—all of His creation, although He despises acts of sin. His will is that all mankind surrenders and receives eternal life.

Surrender your life to Jesus today. If you believe that Jesus is the Son of God who died and was raised from the dead, then ask Him to forgive you of your past life and to come into your heart and be your Lord and Savior (see Romans 10:9-11).

He wants to forgive and restore you more than you know, but since God gave man dominion over the earth and freedom of choice, we have to extend the invitation to Him. He is always knocking and desiring to come in (see Revelation 3:20).

What Happens After Receiving Jesus?

- You now have your name written in the Book of Life. Instead of receiving eternal separation from the love of Jesus when our mortal bodies are no longer alive, we have a reservation in the Kingdom of God with Jesus.

- You should begin to read the Word and pray and ask Jesus to help you to understand His Word. Write notes to study for those things you want to remember. I suggest an easy reading Bible such a New Living Translation (NLT) or the New International Version (NIV) Bible. An easy daily prayer to begin with is The Lord's Prayer (Matthew 6:9-13).

- Pray and ask Jesus to help you find a church that teaches God's truths. It is important to be in a body of believers who can support your new lifestyle.

- Do not try to be like any other believer. Read the Word and live the Word realizing that you will fall short. Jesus will forgive you and will teach you through His written word and taught word. If living as a believer seems impossible, know that it is if you try to do it on your own. Reach out to Jesus in prayer, making your requests known. This is a faith walk, and we will have some bumpy times. However, serving Jesus is the best life one could have.

- Everyone makes mistakes, and some of the old behaviors may not vanish immediately, but if you continue to seek Jesus, eventually you will find that your lifestyle is different, and you will desire more than ever for it to be different. Jesus has given us a way of escape when we fall short: repentance (acknowledging our wrong to Him and to ourselves, and turning away from the error and asking Jesus to forgive us.) If we are sincere in our requests, then we can believe in our hearts that we are forgiven.

- Surround yourself with strong believers, not religious people full of judgmental attitudes who are always pointing the finger at others and are full of do's and don'ts. Jesus does care about our lifestyle, but change will come. We make every effort to avoid, to turn away from temptations, but when we fall, we get back up quickly through repentance.

- It is important to note that the Spirit of

God brings conviction—we become a-ware of our wrongs and realize we are wrong. The evil one brings condemnation or guilt/shame, feeling unworthy, desiring to hide, feeling like you will never get it right, a desire to give up, and so many other negative feelings.

- As long as we live on the earth, we will face temptations, and we will have some wrong thinking and wrong deeds. Just don't allow the evil one to trick you into hiding. Go to Jesus with it, no matter how many times and no matter what the matter is. You are building spiritual character and growing in Jesus. The more you can acknowledge to Jesus your wrongs and seek help from Him to make things right, the stronger you will become in the faith. Jesus forgives us easily. He is not like us. He does not keep record of our wrongs when we are truly sorry in repentance but blots them out (see Isaiah 43.25).

Conclusion

Jesus said that the first and greatest commandment is to "'love the Lord your God with all your heart and with all your soul and with all your mind.'" (Matthew 22:37 NIV). The second is to "love your neighbor as yourself'" (Matthew 22:39 NIV). Your "neighbor" is every person God created, which makes it humanly impossible to fulfill this commandment without Jesus imparting His special love in our hearts.

Bitterness and unforgiveness are enemies to Jesus. He is all about LOVE. Those who confess Jesus as Lord are given a mandate to forgive no matter what. We cannot seek Jesus for forgiveness for our wrongs and not open our hearts to actively forgive others who we feel have done wrong to us. "If you do not forgive others their sins, your Father will not forgive your sins" (Matthew 6:15 NIV).

Epilogue

I reiterate Romans 8:28: "And we know that all things work together for good to them that love God, to them who are the called according to his purpose." To me that means, for true believers, that whatever circumstances we incur in this life, good or bad, a positive will develop from it, during it, and/or in spite of it even if we are never aware of the outcome. I expect to experience Jesus on the mountains in my life and in the valleys, and in doing so positively affect others.

If you have given your heart to Jesus and are now a believer, or if you are a veteran believer, get busy. Take an active role in the harvest. Pray for souls to enter the Kingdom of God. Everyone is not called to be a teacher, preacher, or apostle or the like, but every believer is called to reflect the love of Jesus in some way. Seek the Lord about His charge for you. Get excited about being a part of the Kingdom of God!